DESIGN IN FOCUS

THE DESIGN PROCESS

David Wise

Wayland

Design in Focus

The Design Process
Graphic Design
Materials in Design
Design Technology

Editors: Hazel Songhurst and Joan Walters
Series Designer: Burgess-Rose Design
Book Designer: Ross George

First published in 1990 by
Wayland (Publishers) Ltd
61 Western Road, Hove
East Sussex, BN3 1JD, England

British Library Cataloguing in Publication Data
Wise, David
The design process.
1. Design
I. Title II. Series
745.4

ISBN 1–85210–743–X

Typeset by L. George and R. Gibbs, Wayland
Printed in Italy by Rotolito Lombardo, Milan
Bound by A.G.M., France

Contents

WELCOME TO THE DESIGN PROCESS

This photograph is a good example of what 'design' is all about. Things have been chosen to complement one another in a black and white theme. Everything has been through the Design Process: the table, the chair, the clothes, the carpet and the curtains.

In this book we will be focusing our attention on design and trying to discover what it is, why it is so important and how it affects us.

We are surrounded by design. Everything has been designed, either by human beings or by nature. For all of us, designing is an everyday activity. When we choose the clothes we want to wear we are designing our appearance. The clothes we choose will have been designed, so will the shop where they were bought. This book has been designed to look attractive and be interesting to read. It has also been designed in order to involve the reader in the Design Process – the different stages of designing and making. The Design Process involves two major activities:

1. It makes us THINK.

THINK

2. It makes us ACT.

ACT

Of all the various activities we can become involved in when we work in design, THINKING and DOING are the two most important.

Human beings have been designing and making things for thousands of years. Our existence has been dependent on our ability to design and make shelters, clothes, tools and weapons which have enabled us to protect and feed ourselves. To survive, we have had to overcome many problems.

Design is about problem solving. It is concerned with looking at the kind of problems which affect the way we organize our lives or which influence the environment in which we live. Using the Design Process will help us to find solutions to some of these problems. It is a logical approach to dealing with problems in stages:

1. Identify the problem.
2. Investigate and design possible solutions.
3. Make the chosen design.
4. Test the results.

To arrive at a solution , it is necessary to ask and answer many questions:
What do I need? How will I make it? What form will it take? Is it a worthwhile project? Is there a better solution?
It is necessary to learn new skills:
How to observe and analyse; how to record and communicate ideas; how to use tools and materials; how to test and evaluate; how to work with others as part of a team; how to make decisions.

This book cannot tell you absolutely everything about design, but it will make you think and encourage you to act in helping to design a better world.

Right *These tools and weapons helped our prehistoric ancestors to survive.*

DESIGN IN NATURE

Design in nature is a process of evolution as all living things adapt to the needs and conditions of life. Nature is the most powerful force in the design of the world. Nature has designed or influenced the form of everything we see around us - every plant and animal, including humans, reflects design in nature.

The variety of wildlife in different regions of the world shows the way animals and plants have had to adapt in order to survive. Animals living in the polar regions have developed thick fur coats and layers of fat to protect them from the cold. Desert animals can go for long periods without water, only emerge at night, or have skins which are unaffected by the intense heat of the sun. They survive because of their successful design. The remains of prehistoric dinosaurs are relics of unsuccessful designs. These animals died out because they could not adapt to the changing conditions of their time.

Above *The cactus is designed to store water so as to survive in hot, dry conditions.*

Left *Polar bears have adapted to their frozen environment. They have thick, waterproof coats to keep them warm. Even the soles of their feet are protected from the ice by fur.*

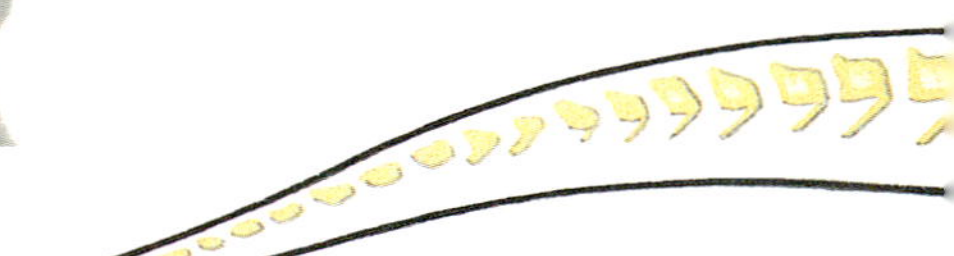

We are surrounded by an infinite number of natural designs. Each one represents nature's attempt to fulfil a particular purpose in the most efficient way. All living things need to grow. In their growth patterns we can find basic features which are common to a variety of natural designs.

For example, you can easily identify a tree by its leaves. You can tell a pine or a palm from a maple tree, because their leaves are so different in shape, size and colour. However, the leaves are alike because their function (how they work) and structure (how they are made) are the same. Most leaves seem to share a common pattern. They are bisected by a large main vein which has smaller branching veins running from it. These divide and split until the whole surface of the leaf is covered by a network of veins. This allows sap to be carried to any part of the leaf. It is an effective design, and the same principles can be seen in the growth of the whole tree. The same patterns occur in the human body, nature's most sophisticated and complex design.

There are 4 billion people in the world and the number is rising every day. We are all unique: our size and shape, the colour of our skin, eyes and hair all contribute to our individual identity. However, despite our differences, we have all evolved from the same human design. Our bodies have to fulfil the same set of functions.

The world has evolved over millions of years and the process of evolution continues. Humans started to design and make things a long time ago, but we are still a very new feature of our planet. It is only in the past 5,000 years that human designs have had an impact on the environment.

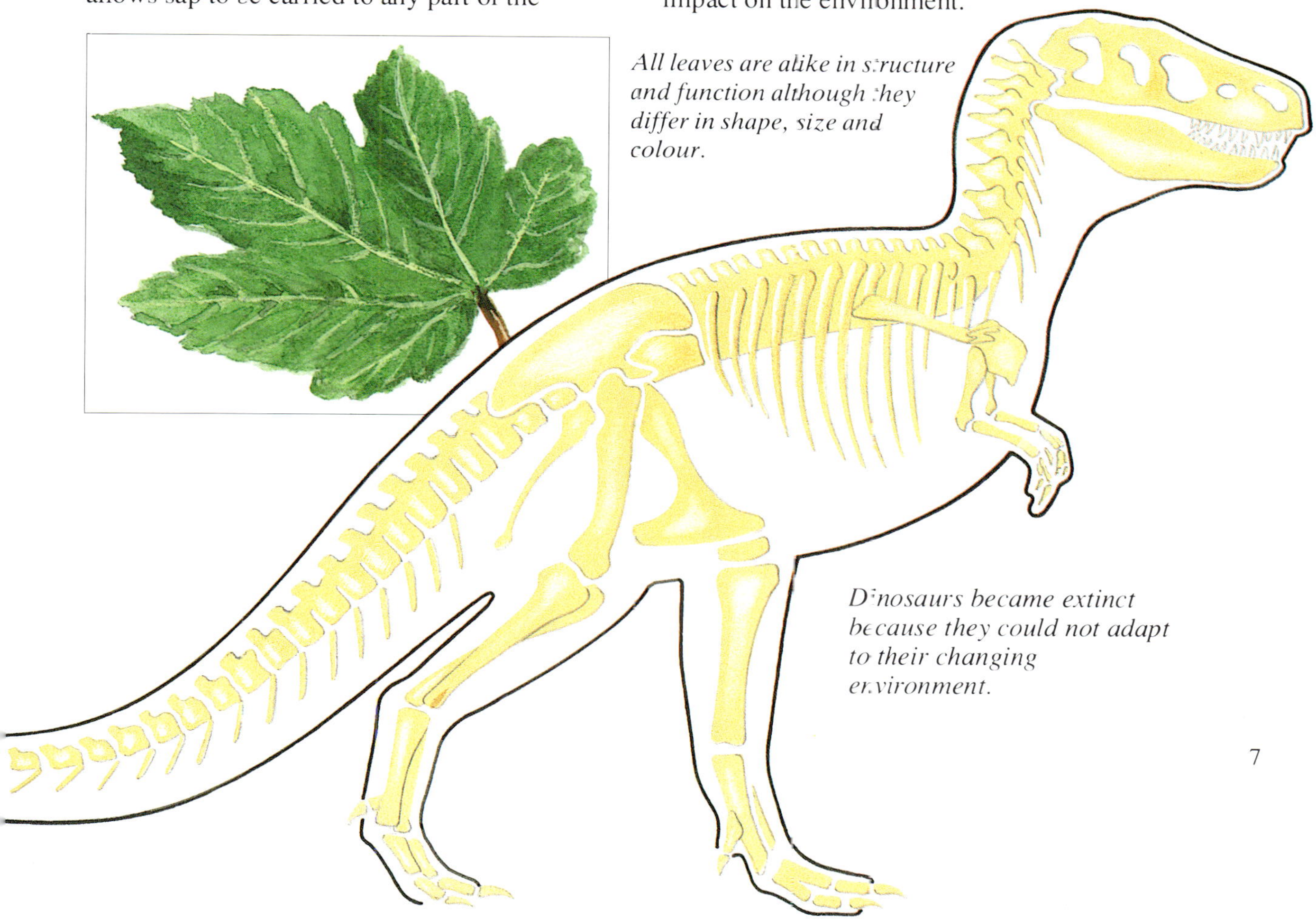

All leaves are alike in structure and function although they differ in shape, size and colour.

Dinosaurs became extinct because they could not adapt to their changing environment.

NATURE INTO DESIGN

Nature's designs are always practical and reflect a perfect relationship between their material form, their function and the environment in which they exist. Human beings, as a part of nature, attempt in their designs to achieve this perfect relationship. Animals and plants survive because they are able to adapt to the conditions which prevail in their environment. Nature has equipped them for survival in a world where only the fittest survive. Nature creates designs which work in relationship with one another. The design of one living organism will affect the design of another.

Some animals depend on plants for food. These animals provide food for other animals and when those animals die, the nutrients in their bodies return to the earth and generate new plant growth. A food chain is established. The food chain is just one of many active forces which contribute to and maintain the balance of nature. Changing conditions can upset this balance and when this happens, nature is forced to adapt its designs to meet new demands and restore order.

All creative human endeavour has, in some way, been inspired by nature. Throughout history, scientists, designers and engineers have discovered, by observing nature, technological principles which have helped them solve contemporary human problems. For example, a spider's web is an extremely strong frame structure. It can support a load much greater than its own weight. The construction of bridges, towers and high-rise buildings always includes some form of frame structure.

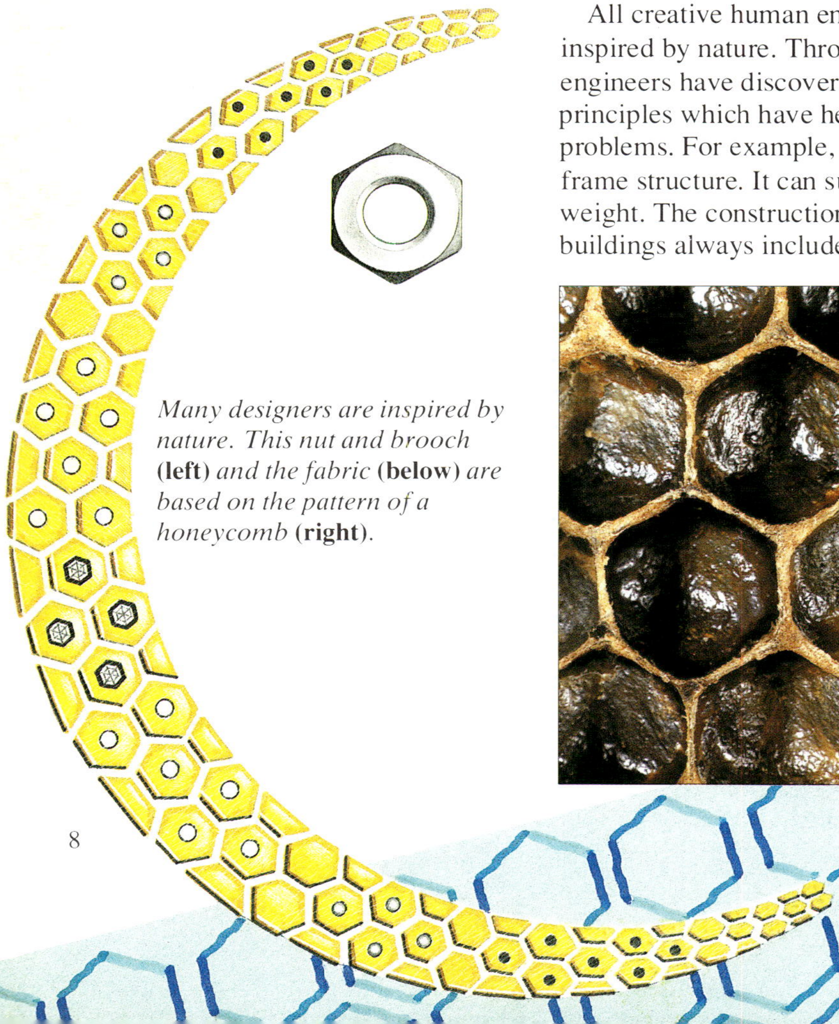

Many designers are inspired by nature. This nut and brooch **(left)** *and the fabric* **(below)** *are based on the pattern of a honeycomb* **(right)**.

*A suit of armour (***above***) protected its wearer in the same way as the tough skin of the armadillo (***right***) protects it from predators.*

Artists and craftspeople have enriched the environment with beautiful objects. Their recognition of the relationships in nature have enabled them to achieve the same perfect relationships in their own work. People have copied many of nature's designs. The natural patterns found in animal and plant life have been translated to design for textiles, jewellery and almost every form of manufactured object.

Humans have also used nature to design much larger constructions. The tubular stem structure of some plants enables them to grow to a considerable height. Tubular framework structures are used in a variety of designs, from children's climbing frames to deep-sea oil rigs. The structure of a seashell is similar to that of a car body shell and an aircraft fuselage. The hexagonal pattern of a honeycomb is reproduced to form a rigid, lightweight structure, used in packaging and the manufacture of doors and aircraft interiors.

In the natural world, camouflage and armour plating are devices used by many animals to deter attack by predators. In our world, these devices perform a similar function when used by modern armies. During the Second World War, the tanks used by Rommel's army in the desert were both camouflaged and armour plated.

The human race has learned more valuable lessons from nature. In an age of rapid technological advance it is important that we acknowledge this debt and learn to work with and not against the laws of nature. Upsetting the delicate balance of nature may prove disastrous to the safe future of our world.

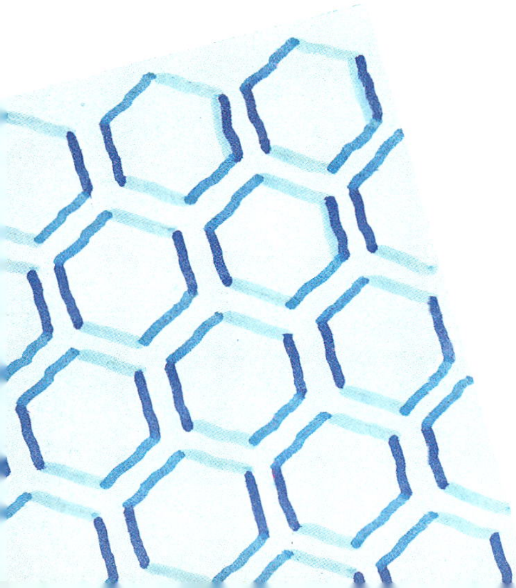

FIRST PRINCIPLES

When human beings started to design and make things, their main concern was to survive. Their first endeavours produced simple tools to help build shelters, catch food, make clothes and weapons to fight enemies. The ability of humans to survive improved as their knowledge of the principles of nature and the way things worked grew. By looking at the objects around them and trying to understand them, humans became better equipped to deal with problems and were able to make use of the resources available to them more effectively.

For early people, every problem had to be tackled without the support of mechanical aids or machines. They had only the technology that was available and the knowledge of the problem itself. They had to start from first principles, working with limited knowledge and resources, relying instead on their experience and sense of logic to solve problems. The ability to analyse and organize resources enabled human beings to work out solutions to problems and so meet their needs.

History is full of examples of the ingenuity of the human race to overcome adversity and solve complex problems. It is thought that Stonehenge was built by ancient Britons as a temple about 3,300 years ago. It stands on Salisbury Plain in southern England, yet the materials used to construct it came from many distant parts of the country. To transport the huge stones which form the main circle and erect them on site was a dynamic feat of engineering skill.

Stonehenge is a huge monument constructed from materials that had to be transported great distances without the aid of today's sophisticated machinery. The stones were probably rolled to the site on a series of logs then lifted by many men with ropes. In 1989, two stones, like those used to build this huge structure, were brought from Wales to Stonehenge by helicopter.

The Egyptian pyramids are a tremendous example of precision engineering. Each block of stone had to be cut to an exact measurement to fit in with the rest of the construction.

The Pharaohs of the Fourth Dynasty in Egypt (*c* 2613 – 2494 BC) set an even greater task. They sought glory in death as well as in life and demanded that their architects provide them with tombs on a scale never seen before. Working from first principles with only primitive tools and machinery, totally reliant on human labour, the Egyptian engineers produced monuments which still stand today. The pyramids of Giza are a tribute to the vision of the Egyptian kings and the skill and endeavour of their builders.

The Greek mathematician Archimedes lived in Syracuse between 287–212 BC. While getting into the bath one day he worked out how to measure the volume of objects. As he sat down, the water level in the bath rose. He realized that the volume of water displaced would equal that of his body, which had displaced it. The volume of water displaced was easy to measure. He also worked out the laws of levers and pulleys and created machines by which a small force could move a heavy load. In this way, by utilizing resources of reason, logic and intuition the human race developed beyond the stage of first principles.

THE GROWTH OF KNOWLEDGE

Curiosity and instinct are the motivating forces which encourage people to discover more about the world in which they live. Most of us have a strong desire to know how and why things work. Once people had learned how to survive, they were able to turn their attention to solving some of the mysteries of life in the world around them.

Nature was the greatest mystery to early philosophers and through the study of mathematics they tried to reveal some of its secrets. Euclid, a Greek mathematician working in 300 BC, discovered a formula which produced a perfect rectangle. Its longest side was 1.619 times longer than its shortest side. This ratio of 1:1619 became known as the Golden Section or Golden Mean and is considered to be perfect proportioning. It appears in the proportions of the human body and many living things. Leonardo Fibonacci, an Italian mathematician working between 1170–1250, discovered a series of numbers which regularly occur in nature. They are: 0,1,1,2,3,5,8,13,21,34... the series can be continued: the next number is the sum of the previous two. When a number in the series is divided by the next smallest number the ratio is roughly 1:1.619.

Above *When a number in the Fibonacci series is divided by the next smallest number the answer is always roughly 1.6190.*

Many living things such as cow parsley, are arranged in sequence. Leonardo Fibonacci discovered this sequence as a series of numbers known as the Fibonacci series.

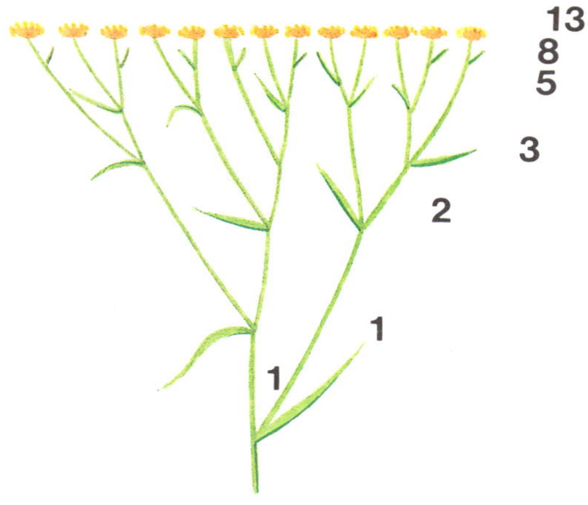

Some of Leonardo da Vinci's designs have been realized into working models for an exhibition of his many talents as artist, designer and inventor.

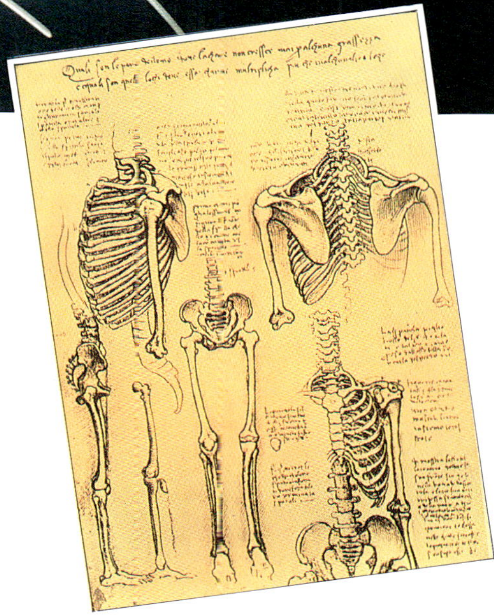

One of Leonardo da Vinci's accurate drawings of the human skeleton.

Le Corbusier, a twentieth-century Swiss architect, once said: 'Mathematics is the majestic structure conceived by man to grant him comprehension of the universe.' He devised a system of proportions and measurements which he called the Modular. He used the principles of the Golden Section and the Fibonacci series in relationship to the height of the average man, to produce designs which, in their proportions, were both harmonious and practical.

Leonardo da Vinci lived and worked in Italy between 1452–1519. He was interested in the way things looked and how they worked. By observing nature, he developed an understanding of its various forms and functions. This research enabled Leonardo to devise solutions to many problems.

Leonardo is best known for producing one of the most famous paintings in the world, the *Mona Lisa*, but he was more than just an artist. He was an important military architect and adviser, producing designs for complex civil-engineering schemes and various war weapons, from flying machines to diving suits. He was driven by a desire for knowledge and was committed to a life of research and investigation. He studied anatomy and performed dissections on human corpses in order to find out how the body worked. He was fascinated by everything around him and kept careful records of all he observed. His sketch books are full of detailed drawings and comments on all he had witnessed and include notes on the flight of birds, movement of water in a stream and the way a piece of cloth hung. For Leonardo, everything meant something and could not be ignored.

Through his work as an artist, designer, inventor, scientist, mathematician and writer, Leonardo da Vinci was able to offer the world in which he lived not just a wealth of knowledge, but a vision of possibilities which stretched well into the future.

THE INDUSTRIAL REVOLUTION

As people learnt about the principles of technology, they developed tools which would make their work easier and more efficient. At first, the people who designed objects also made them. The knowledge required to solve a problem, along with the ability to use tools, made the designer a craftsperson. Craftspeople were considered to be skilled at making things by hand.

The desire for greater control over the environment encouraged scientists and engineers to develop new technology which would harness nature's power and resources. The invention of the steam engine led to an industrial revolution in the late eighteenth and nineteenth centuries. It caused a dramatic change in the way things were manufactured and created a new outlook on the way things were designed. Steam could now power machinery which would produce goods in less time and more cheaply than craftspeople could by hand. It was no longer necessary for the designer to be a craftsperson in order to realize his designs. A machine could now carry out this task. Mechanical mass production made more goods available to more people. It created wealth for many and increased demand for manufactured products which would make life more comfortable or interesting. In turn, this growth in production created a need for more efficient and powerful machines.

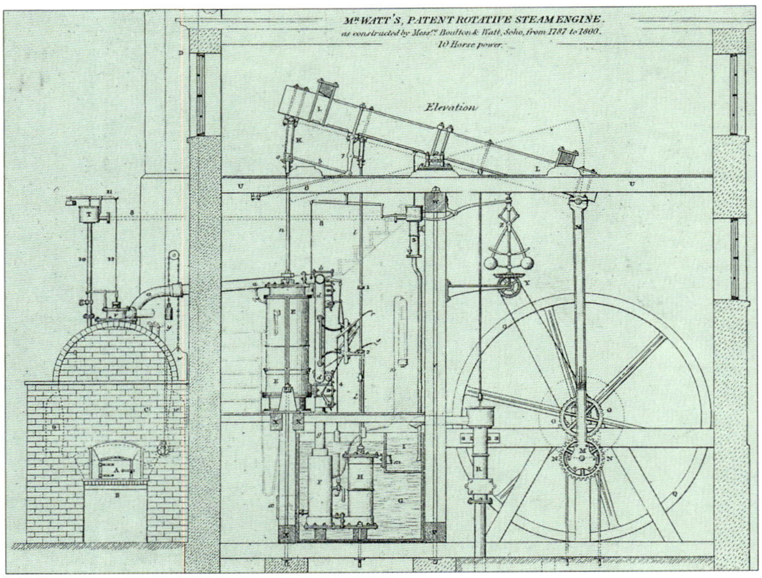

Right *James Watt and his partner, Matthew Boulton, developed this steam engine in the late eighteenth century. It had the power equivalent of that of ten horses. The steam engine heralded the start of the Industrial Revolution which changed the world dramatically.*

Below *George Stephenson built the first steam-driven locomotive to pull coal trucks. This train pulled carriages for passengers and trucks for cattle.*

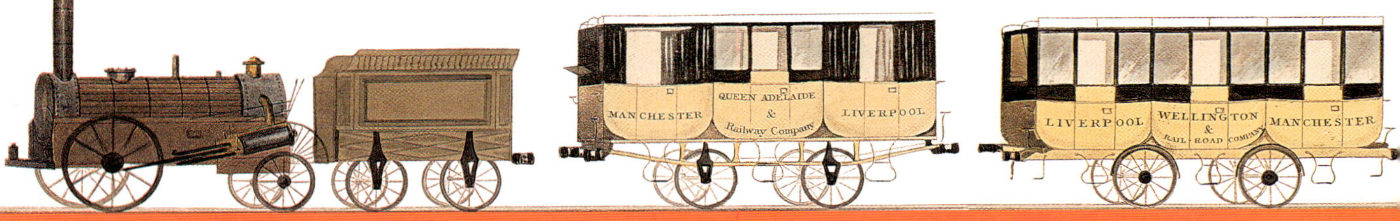

Steamships helped to open up trade routes round the world. People and goods were transported quickly between ports. This poster advertises a passage from Antwerp, Belgium, to Dover, England, then across the Atlantic to New York in the USA.

The Scottish engineer James Watt had produced the first efficient steam engine and by 1775 had developed its use in industry with his partner, Matthew Boulton. Soon, most manufacturing industries in Britain became dependent on steam power and the demand for fuel was great. There was a need for a better system of transporting coal from the mines to the factories. An engineer in the coal mines in the north of England, George Stephenson, designed and built a locomotive to pull coal trucks. The possibilities of moving steam engines were quickly realized and by 1830 Stephenson had engineered a railway line between Manchester and Liverpool, to transport not just coal, but people. His most famous locomotive, *Rocket*, proved that steam engines were reliable and faster than horses. A revolution in transport had begun. Industry could now be provided with the fuel and raw materials it needed to produce the goods for a growing market of mobile, wealthier consumers.

The landscape of Britain was changed forever by the work of engineers like Isambard Kingdom Brunel. He designed and built railways, bridges, docks and canals. He also built the *Great Western*, the first steamship to make regular trips between Britain and the USA. A network of railway lines and canals covered the country and steamship routes criss-crossed the globe. Europe and the USA soon had their own Industrial Revolutions; they changed the world and fulfilled the desire for progress.

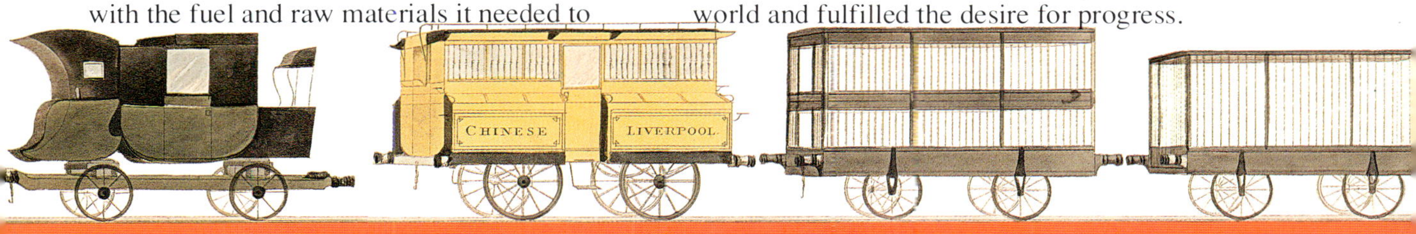

THE CAR IN THE TWENTIETH CENTURY

The motor car has had a considerable effect on the way people live in the twentieth century. It is one of the most important areas of modern design. The German engineer, Karl Benz, produced what could be called the first modern motor car in 1885. Gottlieb Daimler introduced his version of the 'horseless carriage' the following year. These vehicles, powered by petrol-driven internal combustion engines, represented a dramatic new development in the transport revolution that had begun with the steam engine and the introduction of railway transport.

The cars produced in these early pioneering days were based on the traditional horse-drawn carriage and were often built by the same craftspeople. However, the exciting potential of this new invention encouraged

In the early part of the twentieth century, cars such as this 1912 Pierce Arrow were popular in the USA.

Left *A Ford assembly line in 1929. Mass production of cars meant that more people could enjoy the freedom of the motor car.*

Inset *A Fiat* Strada *assembly line where the cars are put together by robots.*

engineers to look very closely at all aspects of its design and introduce innovation at every stage of its development. Each new motor car had many new devices and hundreds of components, all of which had to be designed, tried and tested. In a very short space of time, considerable advances were made and by the beginning of the twentieth century, many car manufacturers had set up their own factories and were producing motor cars: Renault in France, Rolls Royce in Britain and Ford in the USA.

In the United States, Henry Ford worked with fellow engineer R.E. Olds in developing an assembly-line system for mass-producing. He reacted quickly to the growing interest in the motor car from ordinary people. The early American settlers had relied on the horse to carry them and pull their wagons as they travelled that vast country. Ford realized that the 'horseless carriage' would soon replace the horse in all developing industrial societies and believed that, one day, every American would want to own a motor car. Although costly to set up, an assembly-line system could produce goods quickly and ultimately more cheaply. Ford's Model T, or 'Tin Lizzie', was the first mass-produced car and 14 million were manufactured. Ford's pioneering work in manufacture produced a motor car that was reliable, at a price many could afford.

Mass production is the only way in which modern car manufacturers can meet the insatiable demand for new cars from today's growing world market. A few very expensive, high-performance cars are still partly hand-built, but all modern car-assembly lines are now manned by computer-controlled robots. Today, Fiat in Italy is Europe's largest manufacturer of motor cars, Toyota of Japan produces some of the most popular cars in the world, while the USA is the largest consumer with nearly 100 million registered cars on its roads.

SIGNS OF THE TIME

Advances in technology and the development of machine production greatly influenced the look of things. Designers found their inspiration in a wide range of experiences and visual resources. The look of the designed object has changed dramatically over the last 150 years and this evolution can be traced through a succession of design styles.

The Industrial Revolution created new opportunities for engineers and designers, but it caused reaction amongst artists and craftsmen. The Arts and Crafts Movement was created in the late nineteenth century to encourage the traditional values of craftsmanship and combat the rising tide of industrialization. Its leaders, designer William Morris and art critic John Ruskin, said that the machine would undermine the quality of design. They believed that form, function and decoration were all-important in the design of any object. Only a craftsman, with a feel for materials and an eye for beauty, would be able to uphold these principles and maintain a tradition in craft skills.

The work of the Arts and Crafts Movement was highly decorative and inspired by nature and an interest in the art and design of the Middle Ages. It represented many styles linked by a common belief in what its designers termed 'truth to materials' and 'fitness for purpose'. It produced designs still popular today and influenced the revolutionary styles that were to follow. Art and design became linked and started to generate new styles. Art Nouveau was the first popular style of the twentieth century and became established in Europe as the successor to the Arts and Crafts Movement.

This bannister was designed in the Art Nouveau style of which the main characteristic is the use of natural curving shapes.

Below *An Art Deco box made to hold a manicure set. Art Deco followed Art Nouveau as one of the many popular styles of the twentieth century.*

Its artists concentrated on decoration, basing their designs on organic shapes and forms. They experimented with different materials and applied their style to anything from lampshades to shop-fronts.

This cradle, inspired by Bauhaus, was designed in 1922 by Peter Keler.

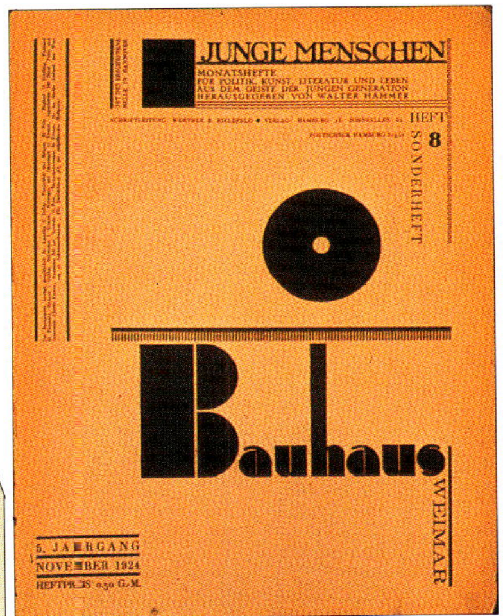

Above *A poster advertising the Bauhaus school of design which was founded in Germany in 1919.*

The Cubist style of painting which developed in the early twentieth century influenced German architect, Walter Gropius. He founded a school of design, the Bauhaus, in Germany in 1919. He wanted to bring together great artists, designers, thinkers and architects in an attempt to establish a new approach to design and manufacture. The aim was to maintain traditional craft skills while encouraging designers to work with new materials and machines. Bauhaus designs were based on elementary geometric shapes, primary colours and simple forms to suit the new mechanical age. The Bauhaus lasted only fourteen years and its designs often failed to fulfil their purpose, but its influence has been considerable and still affects the styles we see around us today. It has come to represent the first modern movement in design.

There have been many movements since which have developed a variety of styles. Each generation has demanded a new style to reflect its image. People want new styles of clothes, new cars, new types of entertainment, even new kinds of food. A designer today works by looking at the past and planning the future. His or her knowledge and skill will help set the style for years to come.

Around the edges of these pages are examples of fabric designs based on the following styles: **left** *William Morris,* **below** *Art Nouveau,* **right** *Art Deco.*

These two radios were produced in the 1930s. The radio quickly became part of the household furniture and was designed to look attractive.

Design ideas are rarely perfect. The need to improve performance or fulfil new functions means that manufactured goods are often the result of a constant programme of research and innovation. Radio is an interesting example of the evolution of a familiar manufactured object. The first radios were very primitive. The 'Cat's Whisker' radio had poor-quality reception and produced faint music which could only be heard through headphones or a large megaphone. However, the great interest and enthusiasm for radio encouraged rapid development in transmitter and receiver technology. By the 1920s clear, good-quality sounds, free from distortion, could be heard coming from radios around the world.

RADIO, RADIO

Radios gradually became smaller and more portable and new shapes developed with the introduction of plastics. This is a 1949 advert for Motorola radios.

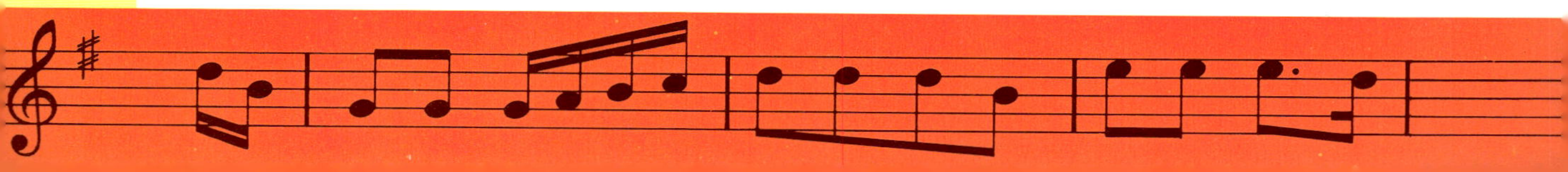

Early radio was most popular in the USA and Europe where listeners were entertained in their own armchairs with big band music, exciting plays and live outside broadcasts of sports and national events.

Radio became an important feature of everyday life. The first popular radios were made with large valves and other bulky components. They were housed in a box, which, because of its size, became an important feature within the home. The radio had to look attractive and match the taste and style of its owners. Changes in radio design were influenced by developments in the arts, science and industry. New materials, new processes and new technology were used to create designs which offered improved quality and choice of styles for the consumer.

Valves were replaced by transistors and radios became smaller. The original wooden box was replaced by a moulded plastic unit in a variety of shapes and colours.

Television has overtaken radio as the most popular form of home entertainment, but radio design and technology continues to progress.

The Sony Walkman *was designed to be worn leaving the listener free to walk about, as the name suggests.*

DESIGN ON THE STREETS

Sydney, Australia, is an exciting modern city. Everything you can see in this picture, from the monorail to the lampposts, has been designed.

Take a walk down a main street in any town in the world and you will be surrounded by design. Every feature of a modern city, such as London, Sydney or New York, has been designed. The architecture of the buildings, the clothes of passers-by even the hot-dogs sold by the street vendors reflect some kind of design which is fulfilling a human need. The role of the designer has become vital in helping to organize and improve our lives.

In today's world, few of us are able to grow all our own food, build our houses or make all our clothes. We rely on others to provide us with our basic needs. Architects, industrial designers, graphic designers, regional and city planners are responsible for our environment and the decisions they make affect the quality of our lives.

By looking at some successful designs and some that failed, we can consider some of the decisions that have been made. We can start to understand the problems that have confronted designers in their attempts to satisfy our needs. As yet, nobody has designed the perfect motor car. Designers are continually trying to meet the demands of consumers for improved reliability, performance, economy, comfort and safety.

Ideas for the first Volkswagen Beetle evolved in Germany before the Second World War, but the car did not go into full-scale production until 1945. The 'People's Car' was designed to be cheap and reliable and was so successful that it enjoyed nearly thirty years of development and replaced Ford's Model-T as the most popular car ever made.

The Volkswagen Beetle *is a good example of a design that met people's needs for over 40 years.*

The Citroën 2CV appeared in 1939 to rival the Volkswagen. It was a utility machine, designed to carry driver, passenger and 50 kg of luggage and to travel at just 50 kph. It was basic transport, but its style, influenced by the Bauhaus, proved so popular that in design it has changed little in forty years.

This 1957 American car, the De Soto Fireflite *sedan, was designed with comfort and style in mind. In today's world of fuel economy and lead-free petrol, this kind of design is obsolete.*

In 1955, Detroit in the USA was the capital of the world's motor car industry. Fuel was cheap and the highways were uncongested. Comfort and style were the important features of American car design and streamlining and other styling techniques were used by designers to stimulate demand in the mass-market. In the USA, cars were status symbols which reflected the power and success of their owners. Designers were expected to satisfy an appetite for large cars and began to follow the rule 'bigger is better'. However, these principles changed as natural resources of oil began to run low, petrol became more expensive and the roads were overburdened with traffic and the air polluted by harmful exhaust fumes. The highly stylized, huge machines, became obsolete and, like modern dinosaurs, have vanished from the streets. Successful designs survive. Designs that fail exist for a short time and then disappear from everyday use.

DESIGNS THAT FAIL

Many early aircraft failed to fly more than a few metres because they were badly designed.

We are surrounded by successful designs. Nature provides us with a vast range of perfect examples. There are an infinite number of organisms which survive because of their particular design. Humans, too, are constantly developing new ideas which create more efficient and reliable machines. Success stories in design are common in an age of rapid technological progress. However, for every successful design there are many more that have failed. Why do they fail?

Nature designs for practical purposes. All animals and plants have evolved to survive in the environmental conditions present in their particular habitats. Sometimes these conditions change and a new environment is created. Creatures which cannot adapt to the new situation will not survive.

The dramatic changes caused by the Ice Age meant that many once-common creatures became extinct. The sea has not suffered the same dramatic changes as the land and has remained largely unaffected for millions of years, with many of its delicate life forms surviving unchanged. However, our exploitation of the sea threatens the survival of many of these creatures. Intensive fishing depletes the sea of certain types of fish. Continued whale hunting may cause the extinction of whales. Dumping oil, poisonous wastes and chemicals will upset the environmental balance which is important for all life in the sea. This type of mistake causes successful designs in nature to fail.

The past is full of examples of designs that failed. Flying has fascinated designers for centuries. Leonardo da Vinci sketched designs for flying machines and helicopters 500 years ago, but by the beginning of the twentieth century no one had yet flown in an aeroplane. Why was progress so slow? Manned flight remained a dream for so long because the technology to produce a machine heavier than air that could fly was not available. Designs failed because they were too ambitious for the technology available at the time. The technological progress made in the last hundred years has allowed modern designers to realize many of the dreams of their predecessors, but not without suffering many costly mistakes.

The *Titanic* was the largest ocean-going liner of her time and was considered unsinkable by her designers. She hit an iceberg on her maiden voyage and sunk with the loss of 1,500 lives. The loss of life caused by the failure of the space shuttle *Challenger* was far less, but its end was equally spectacular. Both vessels suffered from flaws in their designs which meant they could not properly fulfil the function for which they were intended.

The designers of the Titanic *claimed she was unsinkable. They were proved wrong when she hit an iceberg and sank on her maiden voyage.*

Designs also fail because they do not satisfy the needs of the people for whom they were intended. A product must perform well, but also look good. Styles and tastes change. Designs become unpopular if they do not keep pace with these changes. Successful designs become classics reflecting the style of the age in which they were created.

The space shuttle Challenger *exploded shortly after lift-off on 28 January 1986. Many months later a small design fault was found to be the cause of this disaster.*

THE DESIGN LOOP

Identifying the need is often the first and perhaps the most important stage of the Design Process. It is when we decide what action to take by establishing our goals.
Can we recognize a need that must be fulfilled?
What problems will have to be solved to fulfil that need?
What do we intend to design and make in realizing our solutions to those problems?
The need creates a purpose and provides the starting point for the Design Process.

There are always problems that need to be solved. To tackle these problems it is important to clearly define what they are and to ask what we are attempting to achieve in solving them. The problem may be very simple, such as how we dress and organize our personal possessions, or it may be a problem which affects the whole community, such as the design and location of a hospital or sports hall.

The Design Process can be divided into four stages:

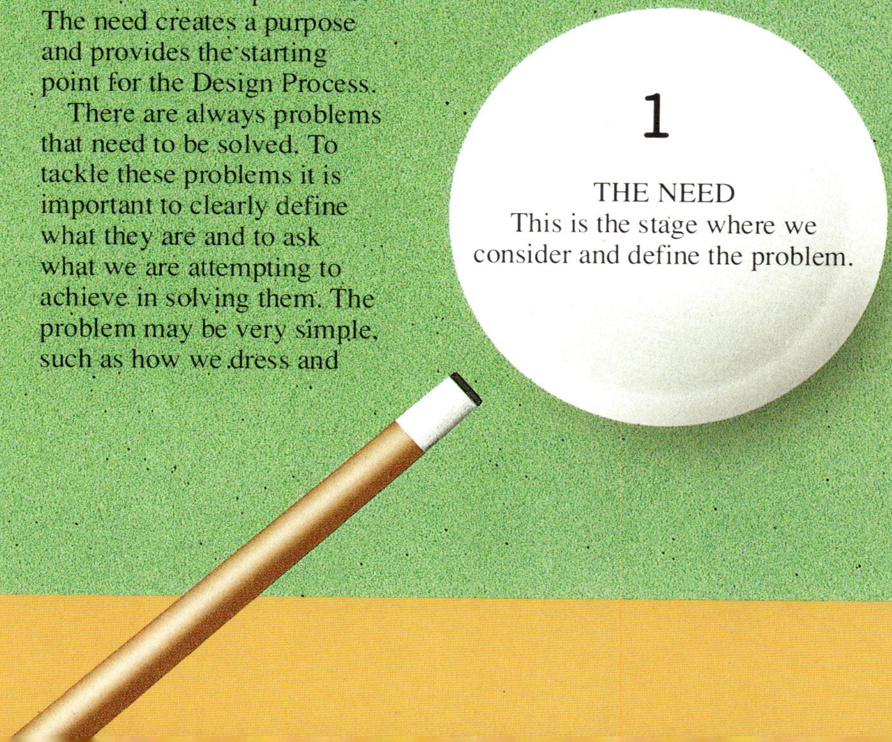

3

TESTING AND EVALUATING

This is the stage where we consider what we have designed and made and suggest improvements.

4

REALIZATION

This is the stage where we make our ideas real.

The Design Process is a means of tackling problems in stages. It is a guide to finding the best possible solution to any problem and it is used by designers and engineers trying to solve real problems in industry. It is a process we can also use, at home or at school, in designing solutions to problems.

In attempting to tackle any problem, from boiling an egg to building a house, it is important to be organized and to do things in the correct order. Results can often only be achieved when the right procedure has been followed. An egg cannot be peeled until it has been boiled and you cannot put the roof on a house before the walls are built. Logic guides us in making simple decisions and the Design Process is a logical plan of action which helps us deal with any problem.

It is not a rigid framework to be applied strictly to all design problems. Instead, the Design Process is a set of reminders of what might be involved. Different problems will involve different tasks, but to find the right solution the same approach can be taken. The Design Process is a learning process because even if our final designs are not successful, we will have a better understanding of the problem and will be able to deal with it better second time around. In this way, a design loop is created.

THE DESIGN BRIEF

Once the need has been identified, it is important that the designer is given a clear definition of the problem. The design brief is a statement which clearly sets out the problem to be solved. It presents the designer with all the information available about the problem and lists all the things that need to be considered. Specifications given in the design brief will vary according to the complexity of the problem. The design brief will not give the designer any answers, but it should give him all the information he needs to find the best solutions.

Below *An architect works on the plans for a new building.*

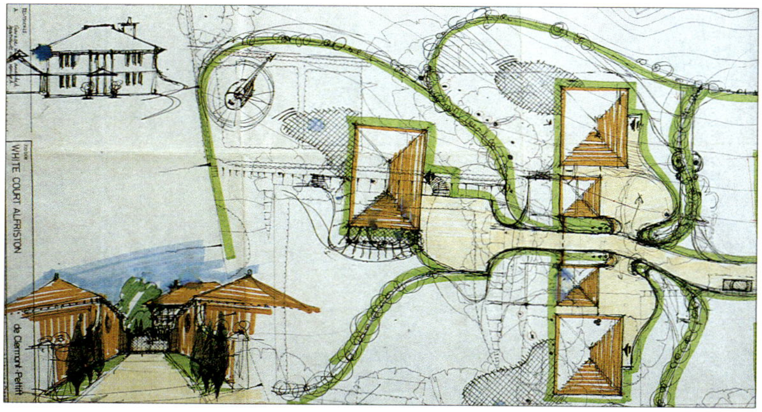

Above *Part of a bird's-eye-view plan of the whole site.*

In this series of pictures the architect's brief was to convert a large, old house into luxury homes and to build other houses and garages on the surrounding land, in keeping with the character of the existing building.

Right *This drawing shows a view of the front of the housing complex.*

At the time of photographing, some of the houses were still being built. At this stage there is time to make small design changes.

Design briefs need to be carefully set out so that they give the designer a clear understanding of the problem to be tackled. Mistakes at this stage will be very difficult to put right later on. An architect's plans must be accurate and complete before they are presented to a builder to start work. Any inaccuracies or missing details may mean the building fails to fulfil its function and could even collapse. To do his or her job properly, the architect must be fully informed through a clear and precise design brief. Only then can the architect move on with confidence to the next stage of the process.

The garages were designed in a semicircle. Originally (see drawing) they were to have had windows in the roofs. At a later stage in the development this design was scrapped and a small clock tower was added.

• MATERIALS • FUNCTION • CONSTRUCTION

DESIGNING A SOLUTION

This stage of the Design Process involves researching and planning possible solutions to the problems given in the design brief. Research is concerned with finding out more about the design problem. The problem will need to be carefully analysed, as there are several important points which must be thought about as part of the research.

Questions need to be asked:

What FUNCTION will our design have to perform?

What ERGONOMIC factors need to be considered? Will our design be efficient and comfortable to use?

What MATERIALS will be used? How much do they cost and do they suit our design?

What TOOLS will we need? Do we have the skills to work the materials? Do we have a machine which will do the job or must we design one?

How much TIME will it take to produce the solution? Do we have enough time? Is there a quicker way?

What TECHNOLOGY will be needed to make it work?

How will it be CONSTRUCTED?

Is the APPEARANCE important? How will it look?

Will it be SAFE to use?

What are the ECOLOGICAL effects? Will our design produce benefits without harming the environment?

A designer's sketch to show how the main components of the front of a Volkswagen car are assembled.

TECHNOLOGY • TIME

ERGONOMICS • SAFETY • APPEARANCE • TOOLS • ECOLOGY

This drawing **(above)** *shows the front view of a Volkswagen car. Each stage of a new design has to be drawn out.*

This research will involve an investigation into all possible sources of useful information. By observing the things around us we might find clues which will lead to the solution we are looking for. The answer might be in one of nature's designs or in a scientific principle. Ideas might be taken from the work of other designers. To solve the mystery successfully no stone can be left unturned.

Once this investigation is complete, the designer should have enough information to start work.

Drawing and model making will help the designer develop a number of ideas and arrive at his or her final choice. The careful development of all the possible solutions at this stage will mean making the best final choice and help avoid problems later on. Once the final design has been chosen, the designer must then communicate his or her ideas clearly through accurate working drawings and plans, which show how the design will be made. It is important that the instructions on the plans are clear, because it might be someone else's job to construct the design. If the designer fails at this stage, his or her ideas may never be realized, because the cost of correcting design faults is too high.

DESIGN REALIZATION

An artist may do many drawings of a design idea before starting to make it. Accurate planning is an important part of the Design Process.

By this stage, the designer will be ready to make his or her ideas 'real'. If the drawings are accurate and the whole process has been carefully planned, then the making stage will be straightforward. It will involve the designer, or the person making the design, in working with a variety of tools and materials. Craft and engineering skills will be needed here, to construct the final design from a selection of natural or manufactured materials. These materials have different qualities which will decide whether or not they are suitable for the design. There is a wide range to choose from. Traditional materials, such as wood, iron, glass and ceramics, have been in use for hundreds of years, while plastics, metal alloys and concrete have only become available during this century. These raw materials are turned into manufactured products by using certain processes and techniques.

Craftspeople and engineers work in studios, workshops, factories or any place where there is access to tools and materials. These can be dangerous places, especially when heavy machinery or bulky materials are used. Safety rules are

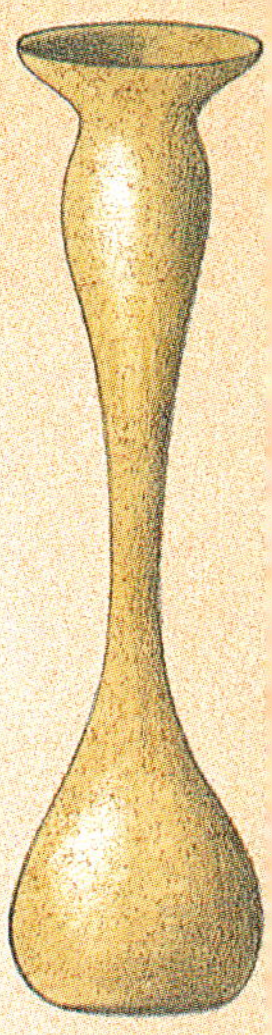

Far left *Having chosen her best design the potter makes her vase.*

Left *Once the vase has been fired in the kiln the final design touches are painted on by hand.*

Below *The design has been successfully realized.*

very important. People who operate tools and machines must watch out for their own safety and that of people working nearby. All manufacturing industries apply safety rules to avoid unnecessary risks to human life. Without these codes of practice many workshops and factories would be unable to operate safely.

A design may be realized by the designer. In fact, most societies have a tradition of designer/craftspeople working for them. Industrialization weakened this tradition, but did not replace it completely. Today, there is a growing demand for individual hand-made furniture and clothes and there is a new breed of designer/craftspeople ready to meet this need. In industry, many people may be involved in the realization stage of the Design Process, offering different skills and expertise in producing different parts of a design. The production of a single motor car in a large factory will involve many workers, each contributing to part of the construction.

The success of these production lines, where goods are mass-produced, depends on good organization of resources. The car has to be built in stages and machines and workers have to operate in a particular order. A single mistake might cause the company great financial loss through lower production output, wasted labour and materials. Designing a production line demands accurate, careful planning. Good design in the organization and control of production is essential to the success of any modern manufacturing industry. The quality of the end-product reflects the quality of the operation that has produced it.

TESTING AND EVALUATING

Below *A scientist using an electron microscope. These powerful instruments are used to analyse and test many things.*

Inset *New artificial materials, especially plastics, are tested at the Institute of Plastics at this Technical University in Germany.*

When the design has been realized, the designer can put his ideas to the ultimate test. The stage has been reached at which the designer discovers whether the problem has really been solved. The Design Process is often referred to as the Design Loop. This is because in assessing the finished product we have to look back to the problem outlined in the design brief and answer these questions: In its final form, how close does the design come to fulfilling the need?

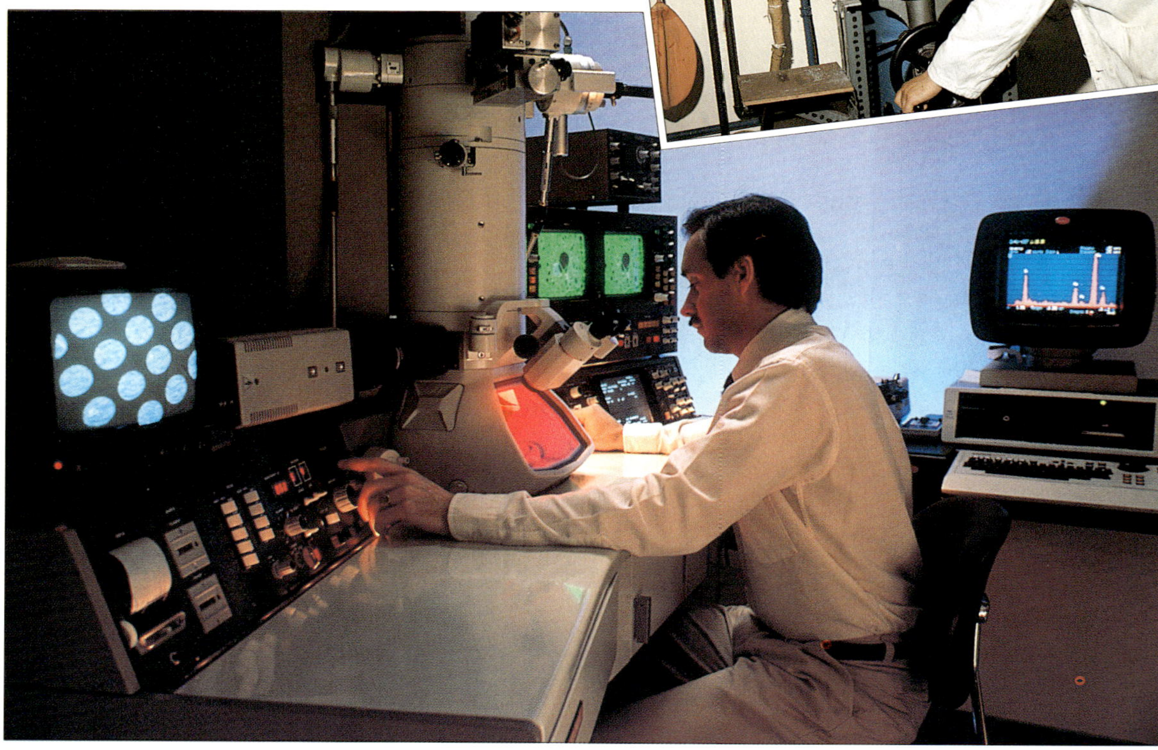

A quality-control laboratory in Germany. Almost everything we buy has been tested for safety and quality.

Does it function properly? Is it efficient and comfortable to use?
Is it attractive? Have the appropriate materials been used? Is it safe to use and in use does it have any harmful effects on the environment? Could it be improved and made to work better? What changes need to be made?

These are questions which need to be considered not only by the designer, but by all involved in developing the design. If a design fails, then the designer can refer back to earlier stages of the design process and reconsider his ideas. Few designs work well the first time and many designers have to return to the drawing board at this stage.
In industry, considerable time is spent testing and evaluating products. Products must be safe and reliable and long-term testing is the only way to make sure of this.

The testing of some products is highly dangerous. Commercial passenger aircraft are allowed into service only after months, even years, of trial flights carried out by test pilots and engineers. Nearly every manufactured product has undergone some form of trial or test. The safety of the consumer has top priority and electrical goods, toys, medicines, cosmetics, even natural food additives, must be proved safe before they are allowed to be sold. The consumer's interests are catered for by manufacturers in other way's too. Companies are constantly evaluating the appearance of their products. Designs soon become unfashionable and a regular change of look is essential to attract new customers in a competitive market. Testing and evaluating produces products which are reliable, safe and that look good.

THE FUTURE FOR DESIGN

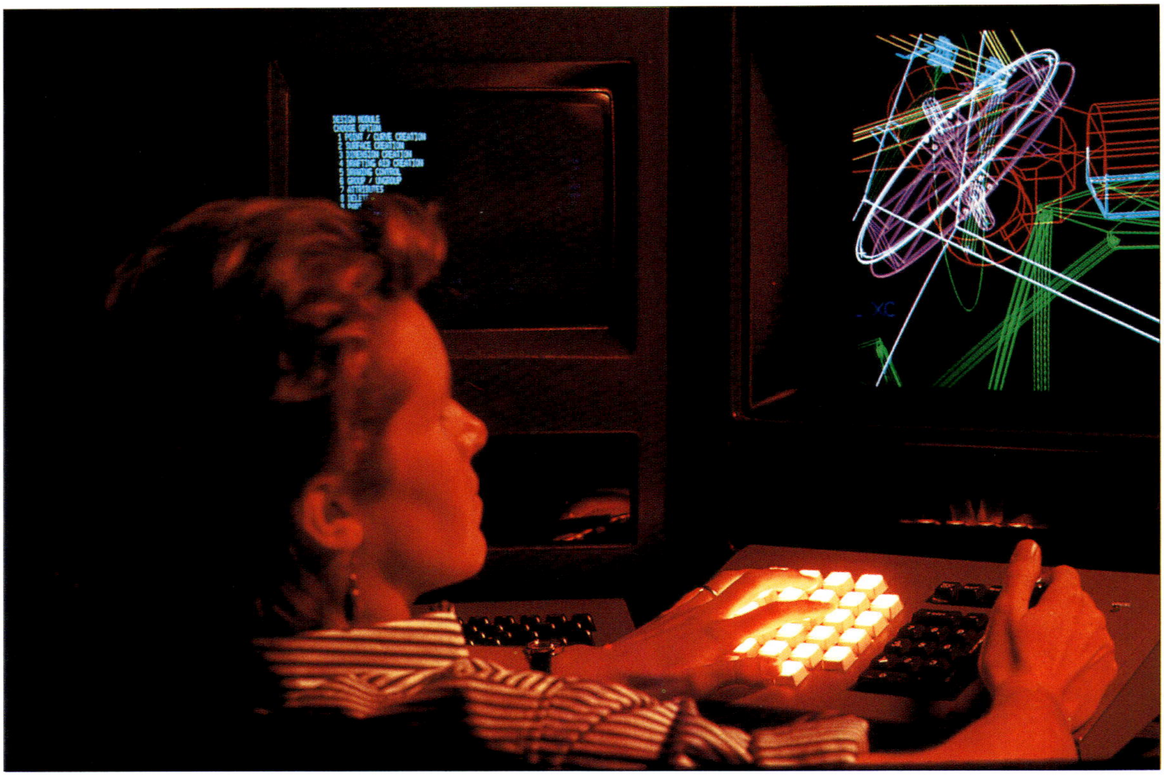

Modern society constantly demands new ideas which work and this can only be achieved through good design. Designers and engineers have solved many of society's everyday needs and life for many of us is easier and more comfortable because of their inventions. Washing machines, dishwashers and microwave ovens have reduced household chores. People have more free time and designers have worked hard to provide entertainment for this free time, with television, video machines, computers, compact discs and more. Design enriches our lives by creating a comfortable, visually attractive and entertaining environment.

Today's designers can use computers to make accurate plans and realize 3-dimensional pictures of their designs.

Our knowledge and understanding of technology has grown rapidly since the Industrial Revolution, but so have the problems that face society. Shortages of natural resources for power and the issue of pollution from industrial and consumer waste have become serious problems which affect everyone, but in particular the designers who are responsible for the needs of today and the world in the future. The role of the designer will grow in importance because society is faced with many new problems. The world's population is growing rapidly in areas where food and water is in short supply. How do we prevent people suffering the effects of starvation and disease in these areas?

The need for power is increasing as industry expands to meet consumer demands. Natural fuels used for power are running low. What will replace them? Nuclear power is a rich source of energy, but the accident in 1986 at the Chernobyl nuclear power station in the USSR clearly demonstrated the dangers of this form of energy. What are the safe alternatives?

As society becomes richer, it consumes more and creates more waste, some of which is dangerous and cannot be destroyed. How can we live with it? How can we make it safe? It is important that we all have a clear understanding of these problems so that as future designers and consumers we can tackle them. Understanding the Design Process can help us create a better world.

A wind generator **(above)** *and solar panels* **(right)** *convert energy from the wind and the sun into electricity These designs do not use precious natural resources, such as coal and oil, nor do they produce waste materials to pollute our atmosphere. In the future, designers and engineers will have to come up with new ideas to meet the world's growing demand for safe, clean sources of power.*

DESIGN A SHELTER

PROJECT 1

The Need

One of the first problems faced by early people was to build shelter. To survive, they had to protect themselves from the elements. Long exposure to sun, wind, rain, ice or snow would not only be uncomfortable, but would reduce the chances of survival.

Above *and* **Below** *Our homes all have the same purpose, to shelter us from the elements, but they are designed in many different ways. One of these houses in Australia was designed for city-living and the other has been built in the country.*

Design Brief

Design a shelter which will protect you from extreme weather conditions. Develop your ideas as drawings then try to make a model of your design in paper and card.

Research

See how many different types of shelter you can discover. What do you think has most influenced their design? Consider these questions (they may help you make a better design for your shelter): Why are roof shapes so different? Why do builders use different materials? Is colour an important feature? Some shelters are highly decorated, not always with attractive designs. Why?

It would be fun to build a real shelter in the garden and test it against the elements. Don't get wet.

You could build a shelter in your bedroom using a sheet, with chairs and some broomsticks. Imagine what would happen in a storm or hurricane.

Try making a shelter in your garden or in the park. Use an umbrella, an old sheet, some net curtains and lots of imagination.

DECORATE A T-SHIRT

PROJECT 2

The Need

Clothes are an essential part of our survival kit. They keep us warm and if we think they are attractive they make us feel good too. T-shirts are a comfortable form of clothing which have become popular and fashionable.

You can buy fabric paints and pens in a variety of colours from your local art and craft shop.

Design Brief

Create a design to decorate a T-shirt. There are many ideas on these pages to inspire you.

You do not have to decorate a T-shirt, any article of clothing will do.

Research

Look around for fashion ideas. There are patterns everywhere, both natural and designed, which you might be able to use. To start, draw the shape of the T-shirt on a small piece of card or thick paper (10 cm x 10 cm). Cut out the shape and use it as a pattern to draw around. You can experiment with your ideas through drawings before working your final design on to the real T-shirt. You will need to buy fabric paints or crayons. These should be available from art and craft shops or large stationery or department stores. A black indelible pen creates good effects, but be careful when you wash the T-shirt. If you cannot get a T-shirt, a plain vest or old shirt will do. You might try your ideas on a pair of shorts. If you can sew, why not try making your own clothes and decorating them? It would be fun to organize a fashion show. You may get orders for designs from your friends.

Draw the outline of a T-shirt on a piece of graph paper then sketch out your design.

DESIGN A MUSICAL INSTRUMENT

PROJECT 3

The Need

People have always tried to enrich the quality of their lives by being creative. We need to express our moods and feelings through art, dance, drama and music.

Design Brief

Design and make a simple musical instrument from objects found around the home.

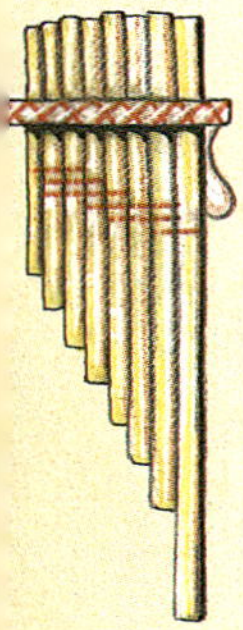

Research

Apart from using our voices what are the ways in which we can produce sounds? Tapping, shaking, scraping, blowing, rubbing. Try tapping different objects together with your hand or a stick. Which objects produce the best sounds? Hard or soft, hollow or solid objects?

Find an empty can with a lid. Place a few grains of rice in the tin. Give the tin a shake. Replace the rice with some dried beans. Shake the tin again. Replace the beans with pebbles and shake. Which produces the best sounds?

Above *Get together with your friends and form a band.*

Collect bottles the same size and fill them with different quantities of water. Put them on a firm surface and tap them gently with a stick. Notice the different sounds they make.

Try banging different objects together. Try rubbing different surfaces together. Tie one end of a piece of string to a fixed point. Stretch it tight and start to pluck it. How can you change the sound? Blowing over the open top of a bottle will produce an interesting noise too.

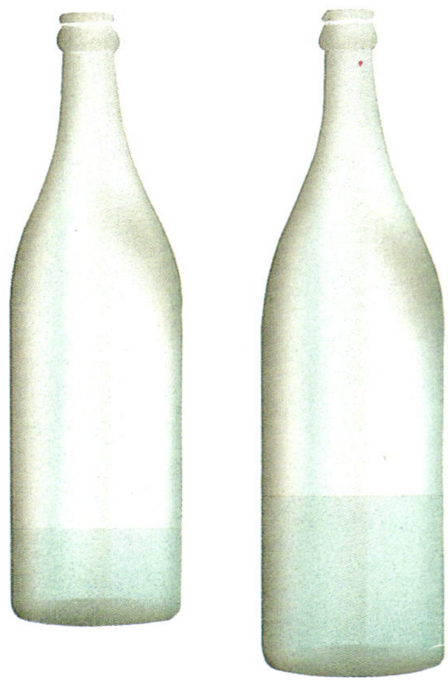

Above *Fill several bottles with different quantities of water. To make sounds blow over the open top of each bottle.*

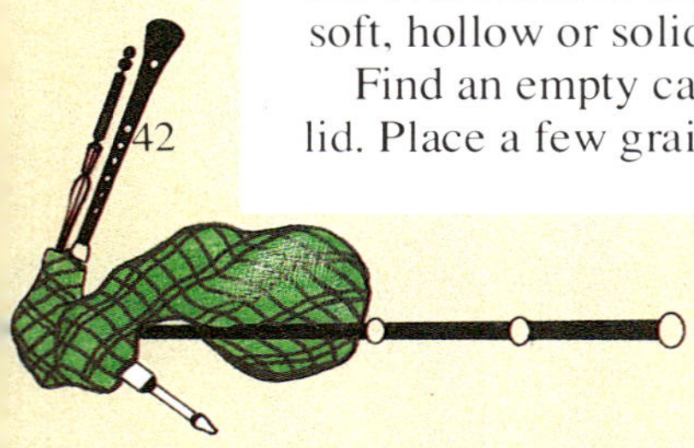

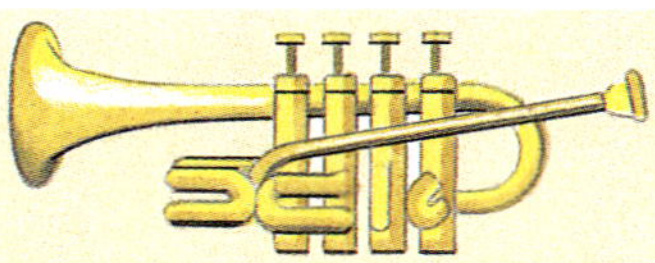

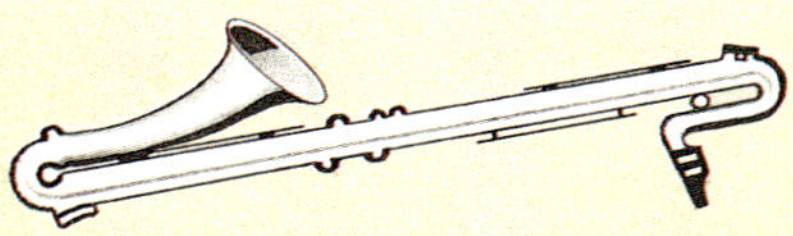

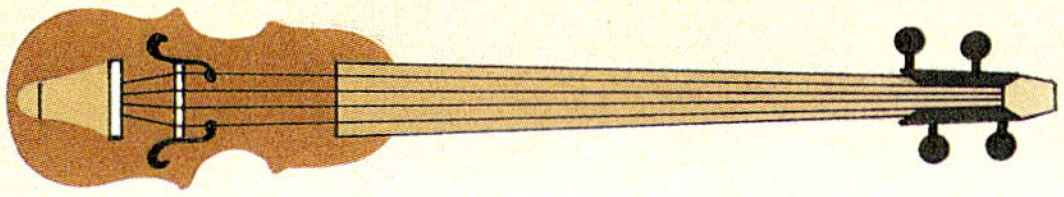

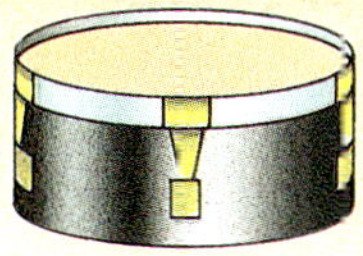

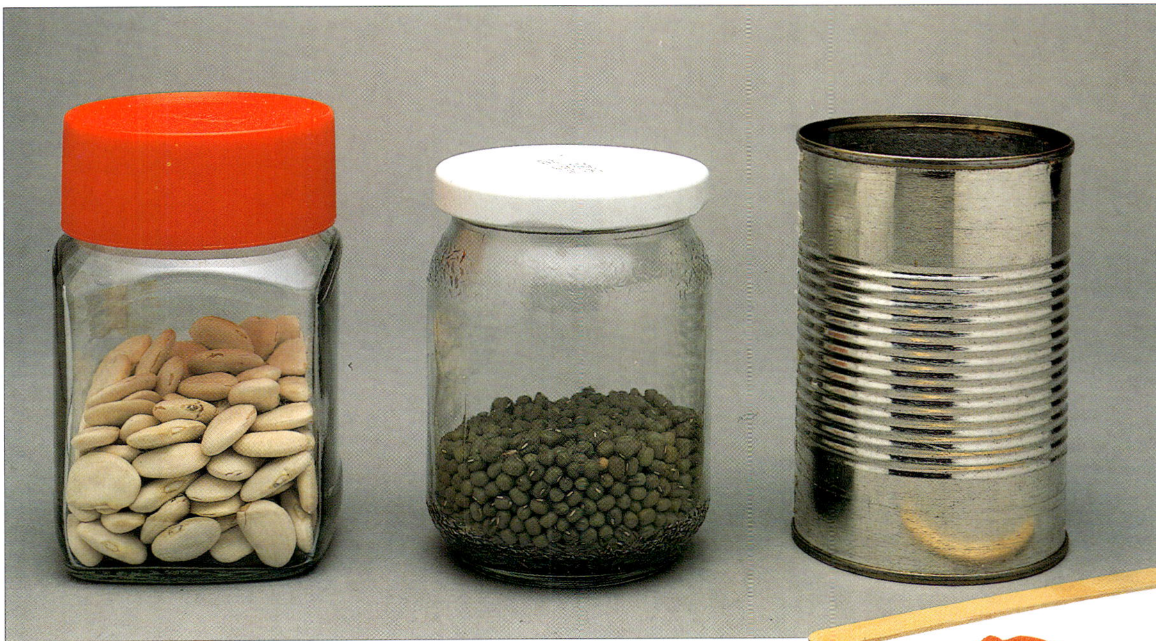

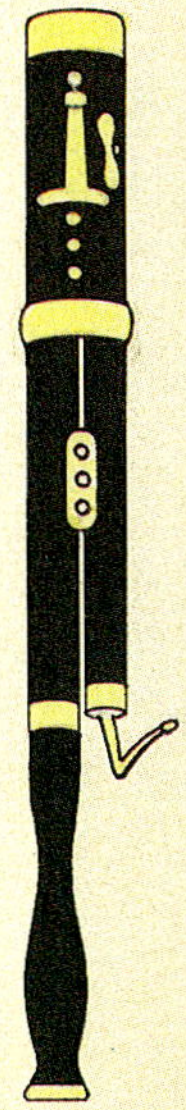

Above top *Beans in jars make good shakers. To make a scraping sound rub a stick on the ridges of an empty tin can.*

Glossary

Art Nouveau A style of decoration popular in Europe and the USA between 1890-1905.
Arts and Crafts Movement A 19th-century group of artists and designers committed to a tradition of craftmanship and quality in design.
Bauhaus School of design founded in 1919, closed in 1933. It aimed to integrate art and technology in architecture, fine art, craft and industry.
Civil engineer A person concerned with the design and construction of roads, bridges and similar public works.
Classic A design of outstanding, lasting quality.
Craftsperson A skilled worker or skillful artist.
Cubism/Cubist An approach to painting, drawing and sculpture in which objects are represented by simplified lines and geometric forms. Popularized by Picasso and Braque between 1907–14.
Design brief A clear definition and description of a problem to be solved.
Design Loop The Design Process. A logical approach to solving problems in stages.
Design realization Ideas made real. The 'making stage' of the Design Process.
Ecology The study of the relationships between animals, plants and their environment.
Environment Our surroundings. The habitat of living things.
Evolved Developed and changed gradually.
Ergonomics The study of the relationships between machines, their human operators and the working environment.
Evaluation The Final stage of the Design Process. An assessment of the quality of an idea or product.
Fibonacci series A mathematical principle often found in nature and used by artists and designers.
First principles Working from first principles means working with limited knowledge and resources, relying instead on one's own experience and sense of logic to solve a problem.
Form The 3-dimensional shape of an object.
Function The purpose or performance of an object.
Golden Mean/Section A formula describing what is considered to be perfect proportion i.e 1:1.619.
Industrialization The large-scale manufacture of commercial goods.
Internal-combustion engine An engine where power is produced by the combustion of a fuel-and-air mixture within the cylinders.
Intuition Knowledge or perception not gained by reasoning; instinctive knowledge or insight.
Manufactured Goods made by hand or machine.
Mass-production High-quantity production of goods by machine or organized labour.
Mechanical An operation performed by machines.
Pollution The harmful effects of poisonous chemicals and toxic waste.
Production line Organization of machines and labour for more efficient and faster manufacture of goods.
Steam engine An engine using steam under pressure to supply mechanical energy.
Streamlining Creating shapes which offer the least resistance to the flow of air or water. Also a type of styling.
Structure A construction that supports its own weight.
Technology The study or use of scientific knowledge to make things work.
Testing Examination or trial to decide the value of an object or idea.
The Modular Theory of proportion based upon the human figure divided into rectangles according to the Golden Section.

Further Reading

Design In Context Penny Sparke (Guild Publishing, 1987)
Design Source Book Penny Sparke (Macdonald, 1986)
A History Of Industrial Design Edward Lucie-Smith (Phaidon, 1983)
The Conran Dictionary Of Design Stephen Bayley (Guild Publishing, 1985)
Design Education. The Foundation Years Richard Kimbell (Routledge and Kegan Paul, 1986)
Design & Technology 5-12 P. Williams and D. Jinks (Falmer Press, 1985)
Design Catherine McDermott (Wayland, 1989)
Design and Primary Education Design Council Report (1987)
The Big Paper Design Council Publications (published termly)
Designing Design Council Publications (published termly)

There are a number of specialist art, crafts and design magazines on the market, as well as general newspapers, comics, fashion magazines and so on, including publications from other countries.

Picture Acknowledgements

The pictures in this book were supplied by:
Aldus Archive 10–11, 14, 18 (bottom); E.T Archive 15; The Bridgeman Art Library 13 (right), 14–15 (bottom), 18 (right); Chapel Studios 9, 32, 33, 40, 42, 43; Bruce Coleman: J. Cancalsi 9, K. Taylor 11; The Design Council 19 (both); Mary Evans Picture Library 17 (left), 25 (top); Peter Newark's Western Americana 16, 20 (bottom); Oxford Scientific Films: G.A Maclean 12, S. Osolinski 6 (right), D. Thompson 8, T. Ulrich 6 (left); The Peter Robert's Collection 17 (right), 23 (top right); The Science Museum 14; Sony (U.K.) Limited 21; Topham 5, 13 (top), 25 (bottom); Volkswagen Cars Limited 30, 31; Andrew Walters 22, 23 (top left), 28, 29, 36, 38, 40, 42; Wayland Picture Library 5, 20 (top); Zefa 24, 34 (both), 35, 36, 37 (both). Artwork by Martin Newton of Sharpline Studios, Brighton.

Index